Discover
Ancient Egypt

by Amanda Trane

© 2017 by Amanda Trane
ISBN: 978-1-53240-2531
eISBN: 978-1-53240-2548
Images licensed from Fotolia.com
All rights reserved.
No portion of this book may be reproduced
without express permission of the publisher.
First Edition
Published in the United States by
Xist Publishing
www.xistpublishing.com
PO Box 61593 Irvine, CA 92602

The pyramids in Egypt were built with giant bricks. For many years, visitors wondered how these giant bricks were pushed or pulled hundreds of miles across the sand.

Some people thought the bricks were dragged by camels.

Some thought they were dragged by people over rolling logs.

Some even thought that the bricks were carried there by aliens!

5

In 2014, scientists, historians, and archaeologists worked together to show that the bricks were probably pulled by people who poured water on the sand in front of each brick. By wetting down the sand, the bricks could slide easily and be dragged with ropes.

The pyramids are tombs for Egyptian rulers. We know about these rulers from the objects, writings, and carvings found near the mummies.

The ruler of Egypt was called the Pharaoh. A pharaoh was honored with golden statues like this one.

This is the Great Sphinx. The Great Sphinx was carved from a single piece of limestone.

Sphinxes were famous for telling riddles to protect special places.

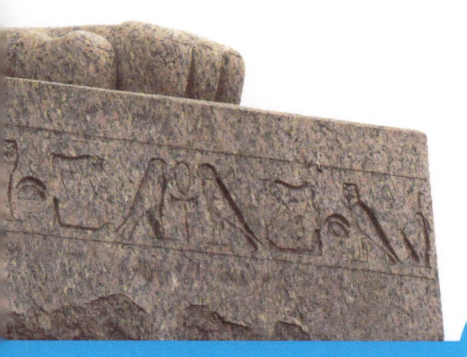

When a pharaoh died, the body was wrapped in cloth to keep it safe and then placed deep inside the pyramid.

These canopic jars were needed to make mummies. The organs were taken out and put in the jars before the body was wrapped in cloth.

The most famous Egyptian mummy is King Tut. King Tut's tomb was opened in 1923.

22

Each Egyptian mummy was surrounded by statues of Egyptian gods. This is Anubis, the god of the dead.

This is Bastet, the cat goddess. Like most cats, Bastet could be strong and fierce or sweet and kind.

This is Horus, the god of the sky, the sun, and the house of the Pharaoh. Horus protected the rulers of Egypt.

28

Sometimes, the mummy was surrounded by animals and objects to use in the afterlife. This is a mummy of a ram.

This is a chariot that could be pulled by horses. It was found in a tomb.

We are learning new things about ancient Egypt every year. It is good to understand history.

www.ingramcontent.com/pod-product-compliance
Lightning Source LLC
LaVergne TN
LVHW010020070426
835507LV00001B/15